JENNIFER LINN SERIES

Rendezvous at the Zoo

12 PIANO SOLOS IN PROGRESSIVE ORDER

CONTENTS

ISBN 978-1-70516-616-1

Copyright © 2022 by HAL LEONARD LLC
International Copyright Secured   All Rights Reserved

Visit Hal Leonard Online at
www.halleonard.com

World headquarters, contact:
Hal Leonard
7777 West Bluemound Road
Milwaukee, WI 53213
Email: info@halleonard.com

In Europe, contact:
Hal Leonard Europe Limited
42 Wigmore Street
Marylebone, London, W1U 2RN
Email: info@halleonardeurope.com

In Australia, contact:
Hal Leonard Australia Pty. Ltd.
4 Lentara Court
Cheltenham, Victoria, 3192 Australia
Email: info@halleonard.com.au

Preface

Rendezvous at the Zoo features 12 piano solos in progressive order so that the beginning pianist can enjoy learning new challenges in each new solo as they explore the zoo. It had been a decade or more since I had visited a zoo but, thanks to my granddaughter Ivy, I was reintroduced to its many wonders over the summer of 2021. We visited the Colorado Springs Zoo and Denver Zoo. I was inspired by the animals and the updated modern approach of the interactive zoo experiences. From feeding a giraffe, to walking next to penguins and watching snow leopards snooze, the time spent there was intriguing, joyful, and fascinating!

– Jennifer Linn

Rendezvous at the Zoo *was commissioned by the Hunt County Music Teachers Association and the MTNA Collegiate Chapter at Texas A&M University–Commerce. A special thanks to Libby Vanatta, director of piano pedagogy at Texas A&M University–Commerce, for her ongoing commitment to the field.*

Jennifer Linn is a multi-talented pianist, composer, arranger and clinician. As a clinician, she has presented workshops, master classes, and showcases throughout the United States, Canada, and India. From 2009-2019 she held the title of Manager–Educational Piano for Hal Leonard LLC, the world's largest print music publisher. Ms. Linn is the editor and recording artist for the award-winning *Journey Through the Classics* series and the G. Schirmer Performance Editions of *Clementi: Sonatinas, Op. 36, Kuhlau: Selected Sonatinas*, and *Schumann: Selections from Album for the Young, Op. 68*. Her original compositions for piano students frequently have been selected for the National Federation of Music Clubs festival and other required repertoire lists worldwide.

Ms. Linn's teaching career spans more than 30 years and includes independent studio teaching of all ages, as well as group instruction and piano pedagogy at the university level. She received her B.M. with distinction and M.M. in piano performance from the University of Missouri–Kansas City (UMKC) Conservatory of Music where she was the winner of the Concerto-Aria competition. She was named the Outstanding Student in the Graduate piano division and given the prestigious Vice Chancellor's award for academic excellence and service. In 2013, the University of Missouri–Kansas City Conservatory of Music and Dance named Ms. Linn the UMKC Alumnus of the year. In 2020, she was presented with the Albert Nelson Marquis Lifetime Achievement Award as a leader in the fields of music and education.

Meerly a Meerkat

Jennifer Linn

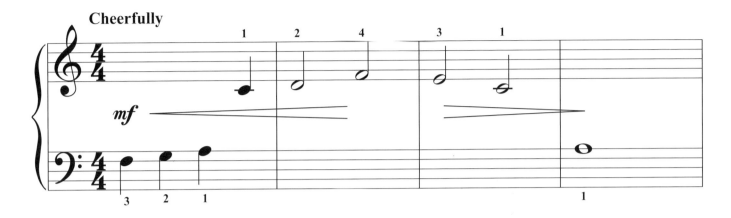

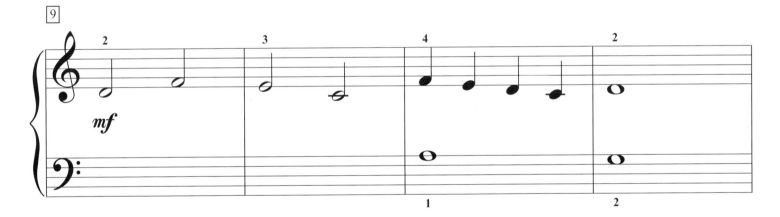

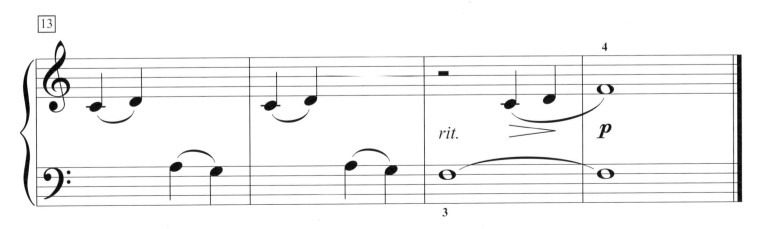

Dance of the Jellyfish

Jennifer Linn

Gently flowing

Both hands 8va throughout

Hold damper pedal to the end

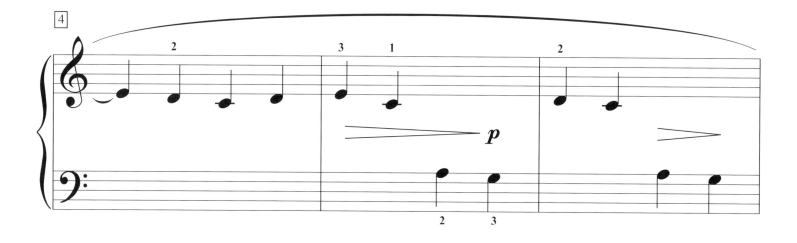

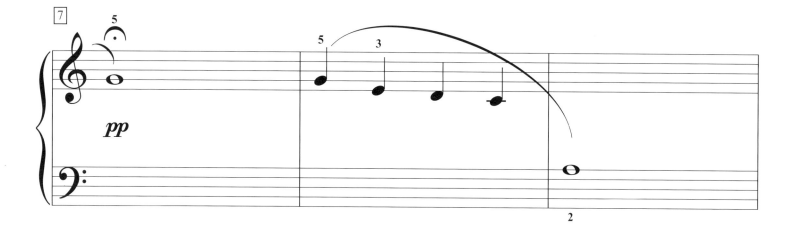

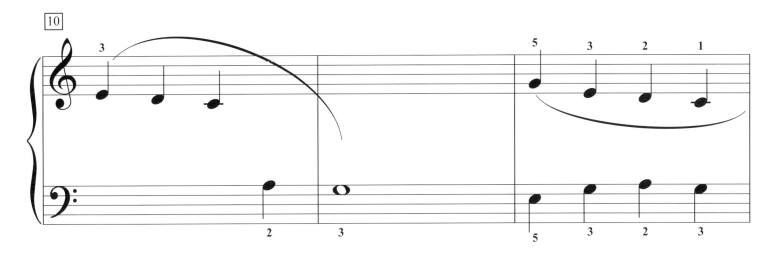

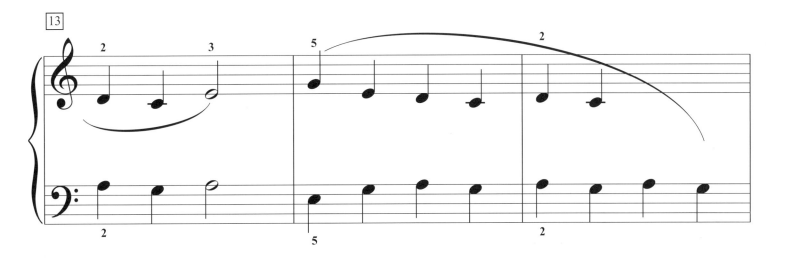

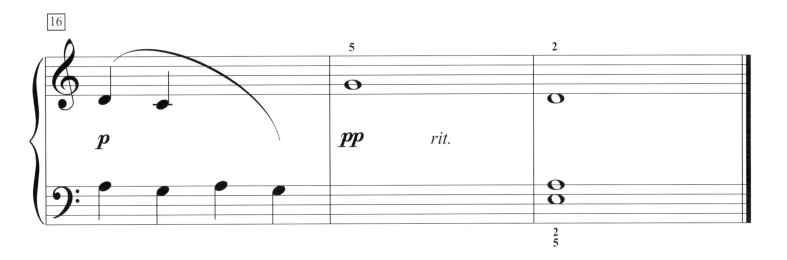

Elephants on a Stroll

Jennifer Linn

Both hands 8vb throughout

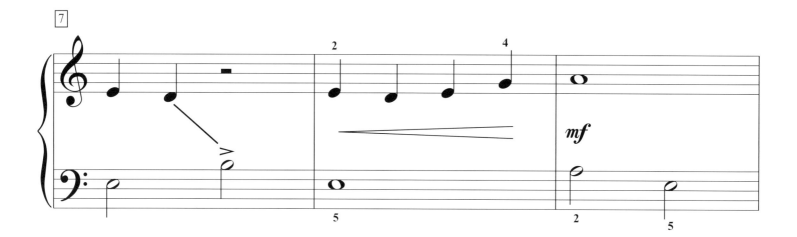

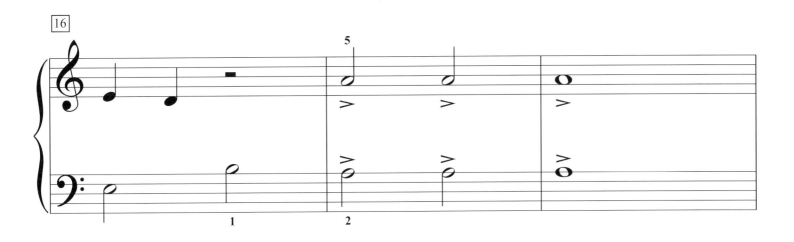

Porcupine Waltz

Jennifer Linn

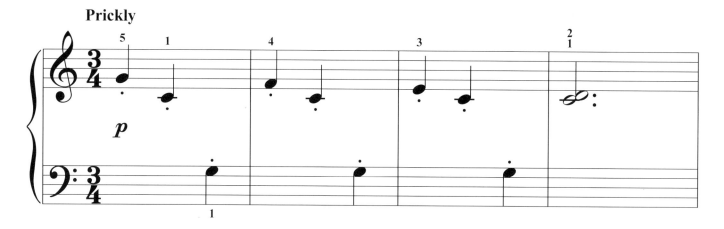

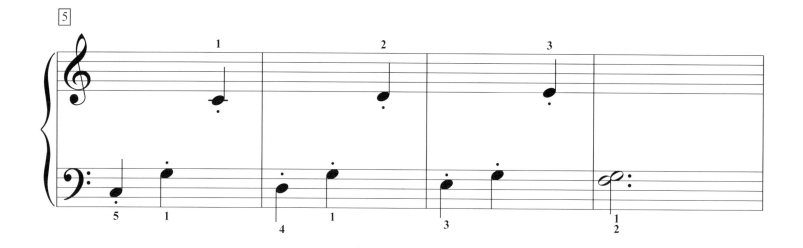

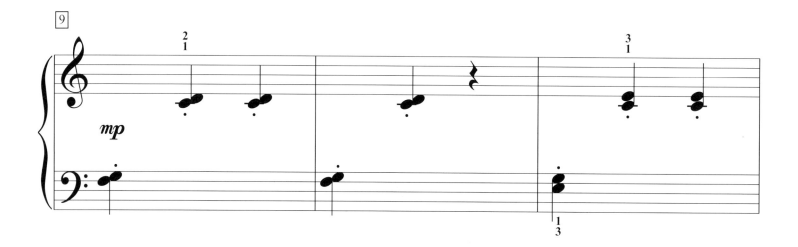

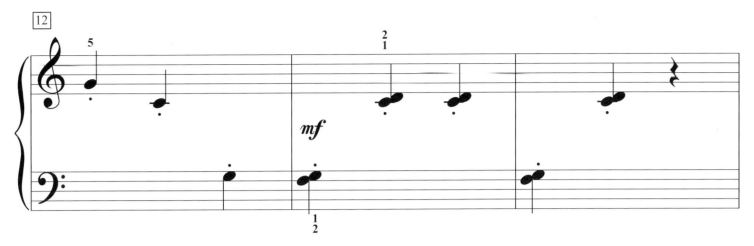

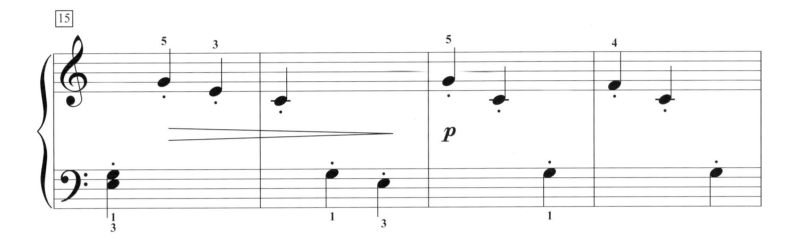

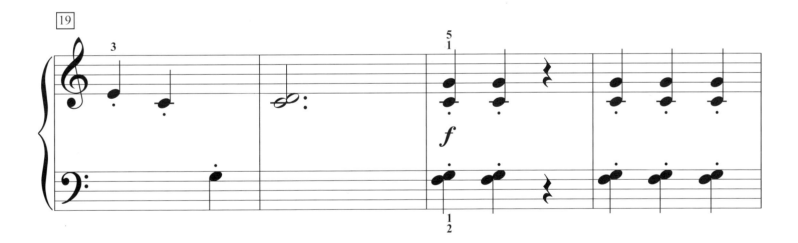

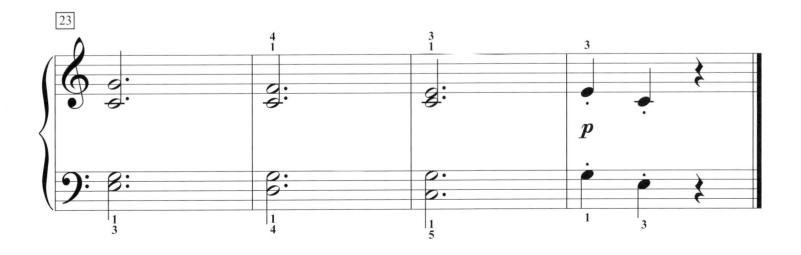

Snow Leopards in the Shade

Jennifer Linn

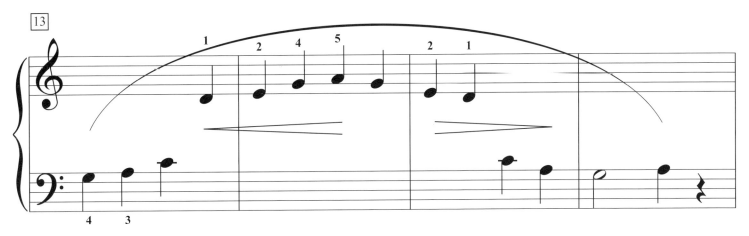

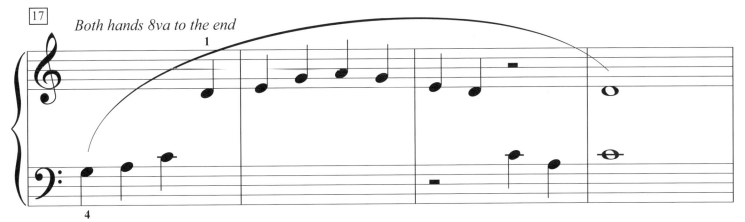

Hold damper pedal to the end

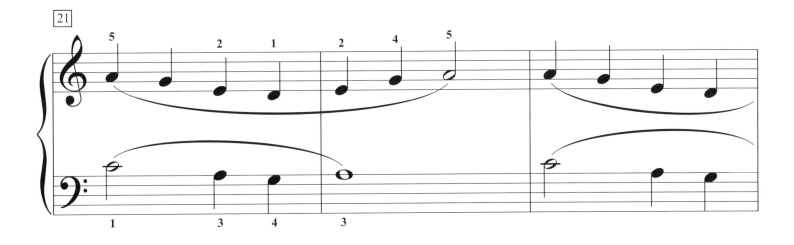

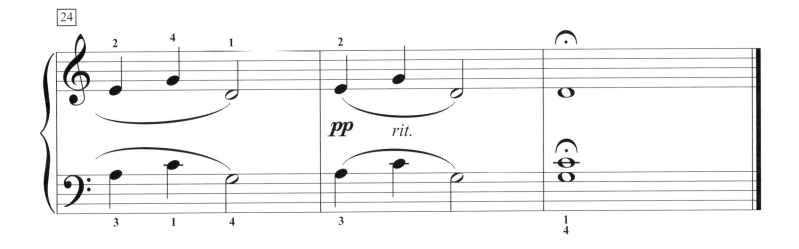

Grizzly Bear Growl

Jennifer Linn

Both hands 8vb throughout

Red-Eyed Tree Frog

Jennifer Linn

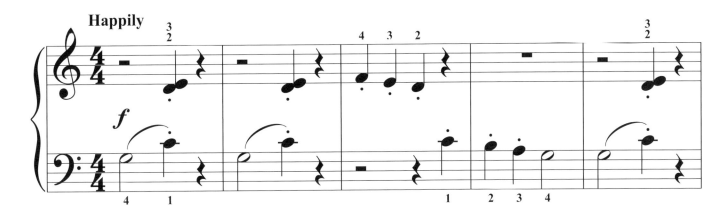

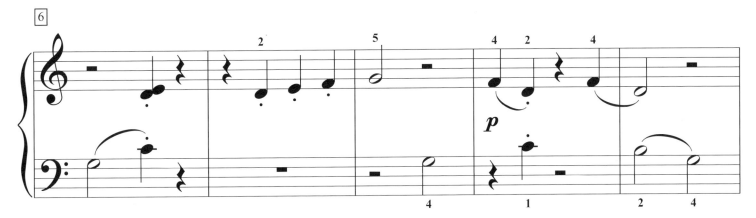

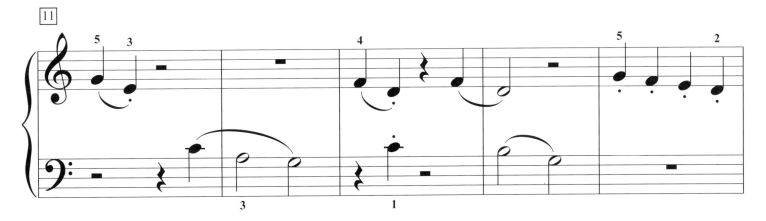

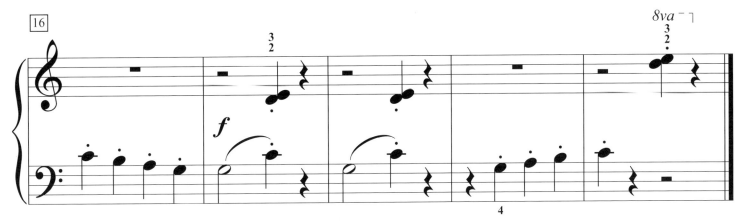

Busy Beavers

Jennifer Linn

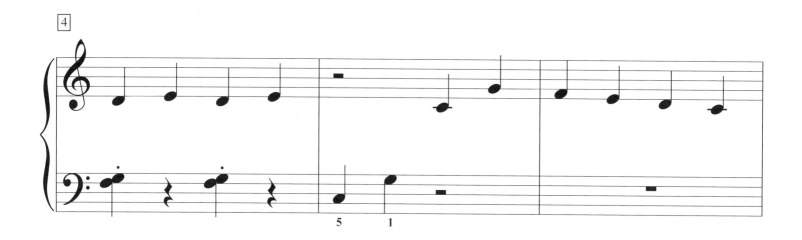

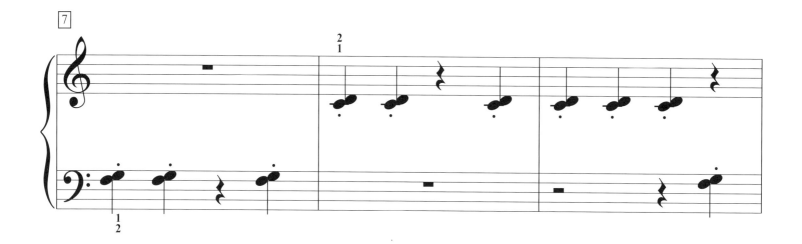

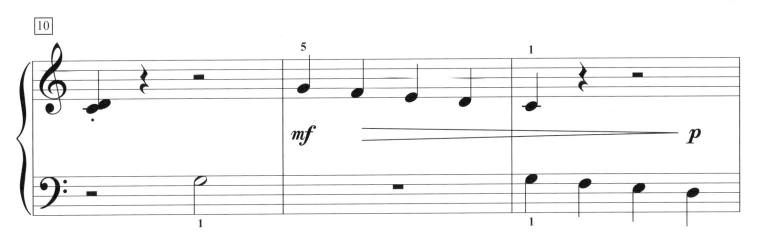

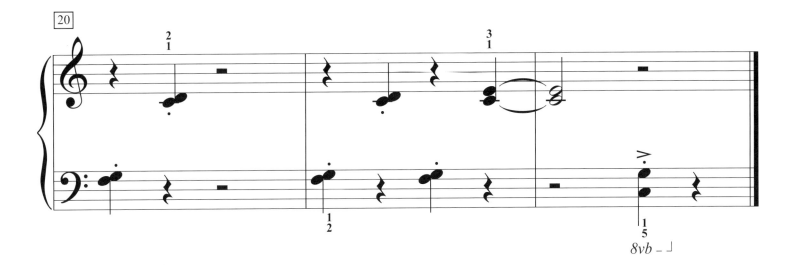

8vb ⌐

Hippos' Muddy March

Jennifer Linn

Plodding along

Both hands 8vb throughout

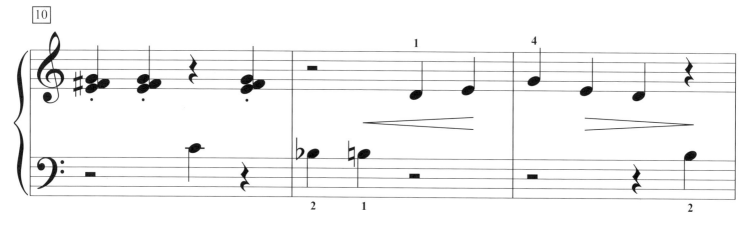

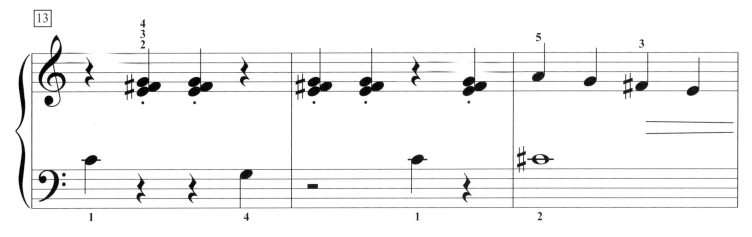

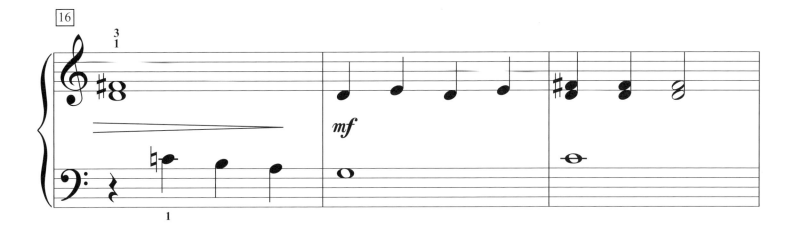

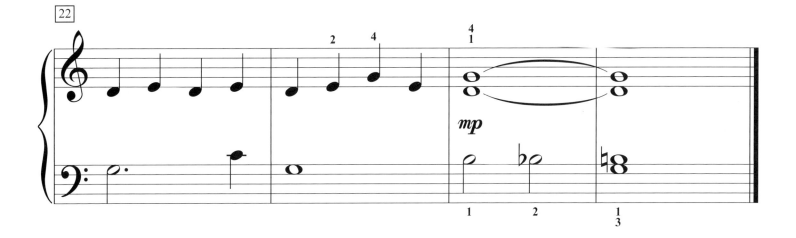

Walkabout with a Wallaby

Jennifer Linn

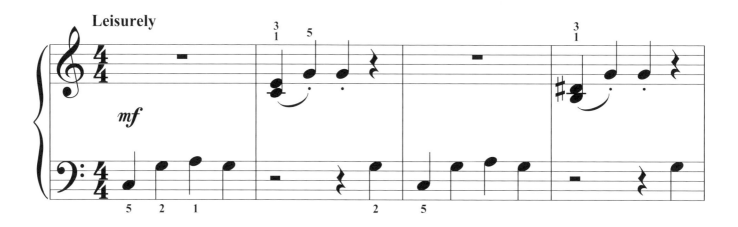

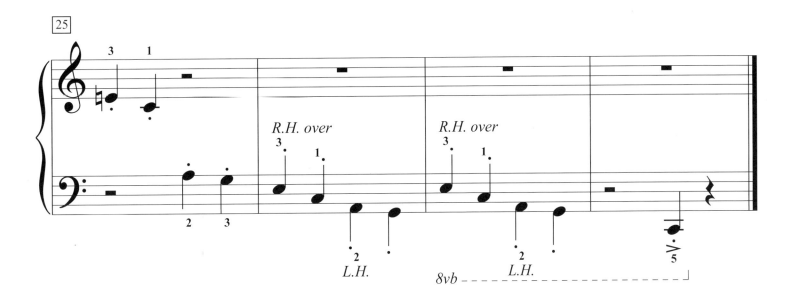

The Penguin Slide

Jennifer Linn

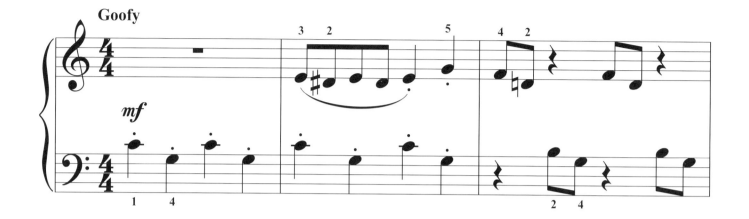

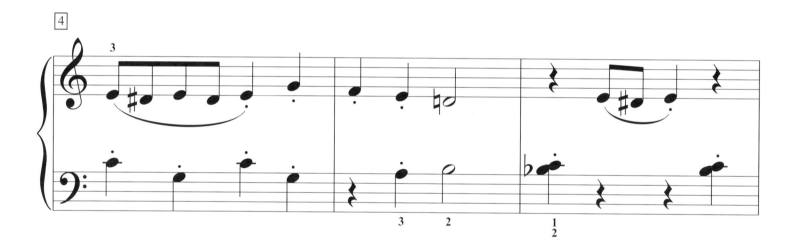

21

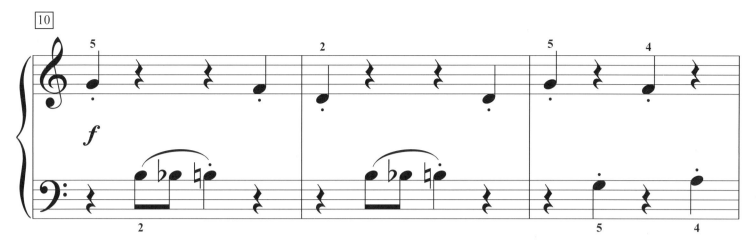

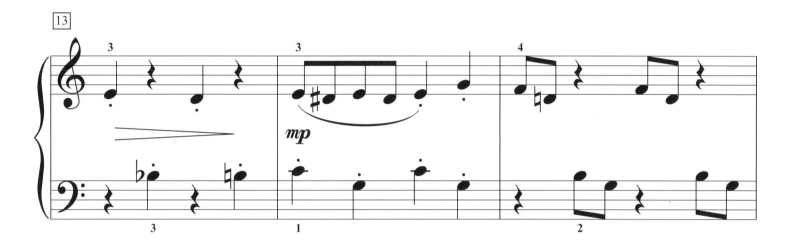

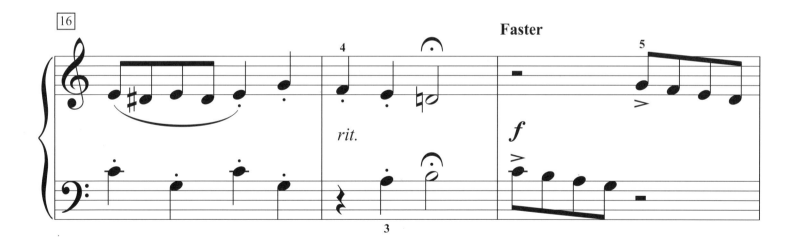

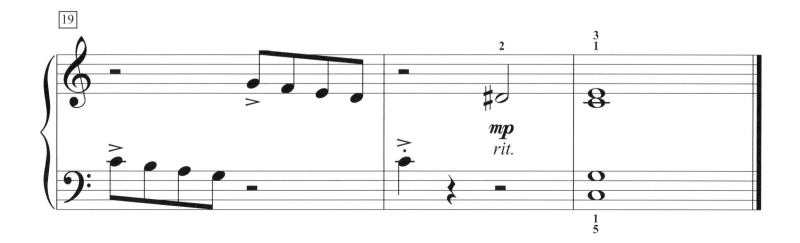

for Ivy

Feeding the Giraffes

Jennifer Linn

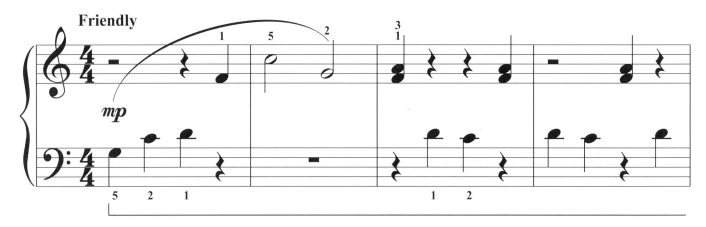

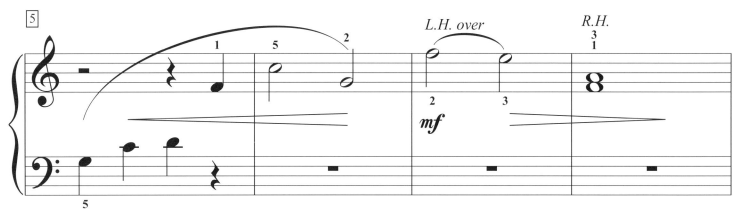

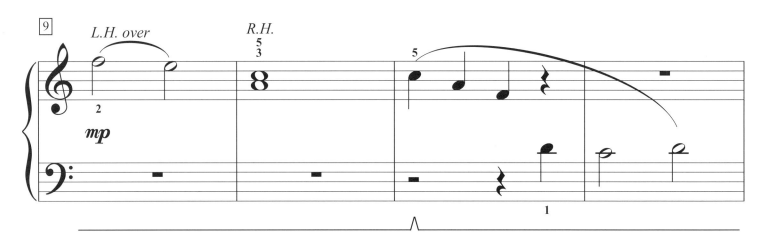

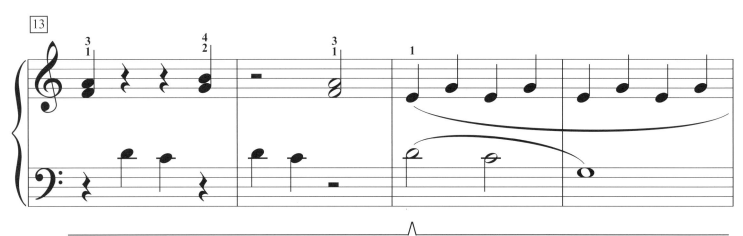

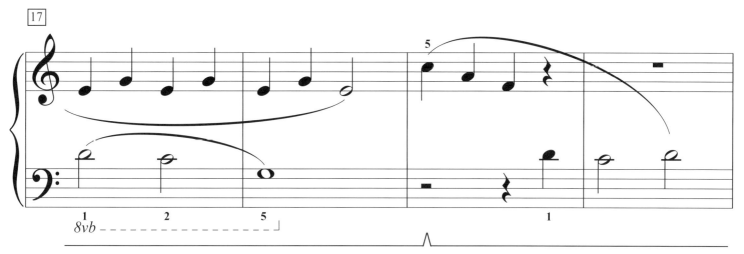

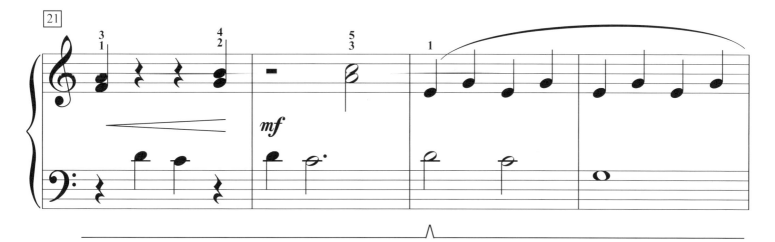

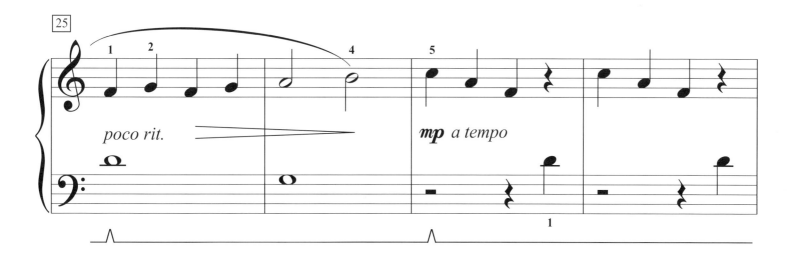

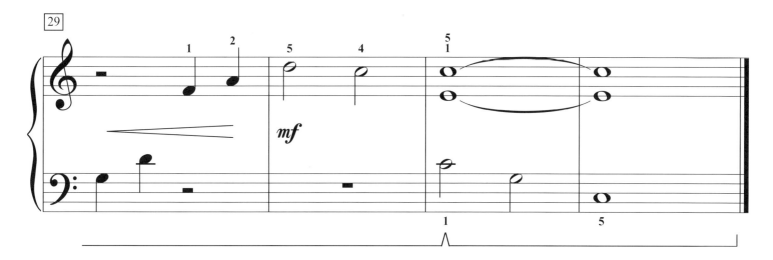

About the Jennifer Linn Series

Each book in the *Jennifer Linn Series* will feature a wide variety of either original piano compositions or popular arrangements. The music is written in a **progressive order of difficulty**, so pianists of any age can enjoy their music with the added benefit of a gradual challenge as they advance to each new piece in the book. The *Jennifer Linn Series* includes five levels:

Early Bird books feature music notation on the grand staff with the note names printed inside the note heads. The font size is large, and the book is in a horizontal format. Optional teacher or parent duets (in small font) are included. *Early Bird* books are designed for beginners, helping them gain confidence in their ability to read music.

Easy Elementary features the simplest, single-note Grand Staff notation in a large font size. This level is for the beginning pianist just learning to read notes on the staff and is printed in a regular vertical format.

Elementary+ books include melody with harmony for both hands and include more rhythm choices and a larger range of keys. This level is for the progressing student who has two to three years of experience.

Easy Intermediate is similar to Hal Leonard's *Easy Piano* level and includes pianistic accompaniment patterns and more advanced rhythm notation as required.

Intermediate+ is for advancing pianists who have progressed to the Piano Solo level and enjoy lush accompaniments and stylistic original compositions and arrangements.